AN AMERICAN ROMANTIC

Also by the author
The Morning People
All The Way Home
Journeys Of The Human Heart

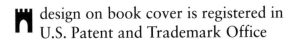 design on book cover is registered in U.S. Patent and Trademark Office

ISBN: 0-88396-416-3

Printed in U.S.A.
First hardcover printing: July, 1995

AN AMERICAN ROMANTIC

the art and words of
ROBERT SEXTON

Blue Mountain Press®

Boulder, Colorado

For my parents, Robert and Irene
my sister, Mary Ellen
my brothers, Peter and Thomas

I do not know the origin of the hope and the longing that have guided my journey across the American landscape, but those forces have been with me for as long as I can remember. They were there in the green and white world of Caldwell, New Jersey, the town in which I grew up. They were there in the dusty wind of Texas, after I had left my parents' home. They were there in the shimmering lights of New Orleans, in the sultry heat of Biloxi, in the storms of Florida, and, now, still, they are with me in California. Like twin beacons, they shine in my spirit, and neither their power nor their promise has been diminished.

Perhaps they came with the realization that I was born in a country where individual freedom was possible, for, very early in my life, I rejected the conformity that seemed to guide so many others. I chose to be free, to live an original life, to experience all that I could and, then, to return something entirely unique to the world.

I had no idea then of the miles and the years that would stretch before me, of the disappointments and doubts that would plague my course. I had no awareness of where I would go or how I would live. I only knew that, deep within me, hope was stirring, and longing had been born.

Now, looking back at all the miles and all the years, I cannot find one step or one moment to regret. Each pace and each second brought me closer to this place and this time and to the work you now hold in your hands.

Seven years ago, shortly after my travels had brought me to San Francisco, I began to feel the need to share some of the things this country had shown me. I had learned that there are people who are so quietly fine that one feels unexpected joy in their presence. I had learned that there are moments that far outlive the tick of appointed time. I had learned that, all across this country, there is so much beauty that we take it for granted and forget to wonder at its brilliance.

Out of the need to share these things, I began to draw.

From the very first I have worked with a quill pen and india ink, composing each piece entirely of dots of ink. This technique is called *stippling.* It is a painstakingly slow method, requiring that I devote between two and five weeks to each drawing. But, for me, there is a kind of justice in this, for the subjects of my works deserve refinement and delicacy in their presentation.

On the following pages you will find some of the examples of the work that has become my life. Deeply etched within each piece are the hope and the longing that led to its creation, for, now, I celebrate these forces.

They have guided me to this place and set my spirit free.

In my art I have found a home.

You, fellow traveller, are welcome within it.

Robert Sexton

An American Romantic

SUNFLOWER SEASON

*I was seven or eight years old, and it was
dusk, and my grandfather sat beneath the
grape arbor, talking low of his boyhood in
Poland. I lay in the grass before him,
watching the sunflowers sway in the breeze,
thinking of nothing, and feeling how fine
it was to be alive.*

UNTITLED #1

*After the union of love, passion becomes a quiet
thing. In silences and subtleties we give ourselves,
no longer to the moment, but fully to one another.
And, if the chance we have taken is understood,
the meaning of our lives begins to change.*

BECAUSE
you lie beside me now,
I dream of kites
and carousels
And sleep at peace
within myself
And fear the night
no more...

TO EACH, A SEASON

*The quality of a life . . . the richness of its minutes
. . . is all that really matters. Only those moments
touched by care, effort, joy and love are
of lasting value.*

UNTITLED #2

Love is not static. Like all living things,
it changes. It can either grow or die.
Take it for granted, neglect it; it will
pass like a cold wind. Give it words,
gestures, expressions of yourself, and it
will become whole and live through your
life.

If ever I must sail from you,
Remember this:
My heart remains
   in the palm of this shell.
I leave it with you,
   for no one else
      can tend it so dearly.
                  You are my harbor;
                  You are my home.

WONDER

It is all around us, quietly unfolding,
ever revealing the spirit of life. The most peaceful
moments I have known have been those spent
in pursuit of its gentle influence.

LADIES OF THE AFTERNOON

Two special friends, Fannie and Ella
never had to be asked to pose for this.
Every afternoon Ella put on her little
hat and gloves and trotted over to
Fannie's. Then, for hours, they'd . . . chat.

UNTITLED #3

We cannot fully love another until we have come to value ourselves. Only then can we believe in the worth of that which we give and truly know the merit of that which is given to us.

Awaking beside you,
Feeling your breath,
I've known
the deepest sense of joy,
At finding my life —
At last, complete —
in the gentle circle
of your arms.

THE FLOWERS OF WINTER

In a time of love, we took a long walk
around Lake Chabot. I picked these, and
we laughed, and the day was so fine that
we imagined we would always be together.
Now, we are parted, and that time is gone.
Only the flowers remain. They, and the
bright memory of a winter's day.

SONG OF THE SEA

Words are frail and temporal here.
Like bits of sand they slip away, until all that remains
is a sense of awe and the quiet release of coming home.

I go to the SEA
for THERE, AT PEACE,
my SOUL CONVERGES
with its SOURCE
and turns its touch
from EARTHLY CARE
and feels
the pulse of God.

TENDER REFUGE

*Mendocino is a gentle place. It wears a
cloak of wildflowers and fog and quietly
beckons, when the rest of the world becomes
close and dry. In the best of times and in
the worst, I have sought its touch, and,
like the most constant of friends, it has
never turned me away.*

MENDOCINO

UNTITLED #4

Falling in love is a spontaneous thing.
Keeping that feeling is not. The romance
will continue only if you give your best
effort to pleasing the one you care for.
For, without romance, love will become
something you used to enjoy.

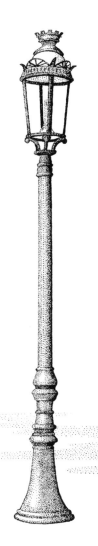

If time is tender
    and fortune, kind,
you and I
    will stroll this life
as if it were a boulevard,
    shimmering,
and we had just
    begun to love.

YEARS AGO AND FAR AWAY

In 1908 Frank Burke left San Francisco to seek his fortune in Goldfield, Nevada. His new wife, Bertha, remained in The City, and for two-and-a-half years their love was sustained by the postcards they exchanged daily. This is a tribute to that kind of sharing.

POST CA

Nov. 28-08
Hello sweet.
Just arrived. Are
you awful & lonesome
without your hubby.
I am some for
you
& Frank

Goldfield, Nev.

UNTITLED #5

*True intimacy is the opening of one soul
to another. No gift on earth can compare with it,
for it touches us more profoundly than our
imagination can envision. When two people
share their lives, freely, openly, without
reservation, it is as if each had become complete.*

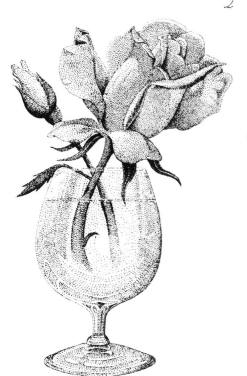

I never knew
that dawn could break
with peace so deep
and hope so wide,
'til that first morning
when I awoke,
and you lay, sleeping,
by my side.

OF TIME REMEMBERED

The brightness of the past is never lost. Memory brings it back, and contemplation brings it near again. Some may deny the virtues of sentiment; you will not find me among them. There is too much of the past that I do not wish to forget.

SUNDAY MORNING: SANTA FE

*From Florida through Texas, late-summer storms battered
my car and darkened my hope for a new life in California.
Then, as I crossed into New Mexico, the sky seemed to break,
and the sun with dazzling suddenness poured down.
Like the steaming mist on the road ahead, my spirits rose,
and I felt the promise of what lay beyond.*

UNTITLED #6

There is a special quality to the hours we pass with those we care for. Like the light of dusk, it lingers long after the moment itself is gone. Those who have become dear to us should never be denied the knowledge of how deeply they have touched our lives.

The time we share
is never spent.
It lives in memory
and brightens all the days
that follow.
Because you are here
my life is richer
than I ever dared to hope
or chanced to dream.

IN TRIBUTE TO LOREN EISELEY

*This man was more responsible for the
formation of my own philosophy than any
other. If you do not yet know of him,
seek out THE IMMENSE JOURNEY at your
library or bookstore. If you have shared
his thoughts, you will understand the reason
for this tribute.*

On this earth
    there are other worlds.
Study them,
    and you will begin to know
    the wonders
    of our own.

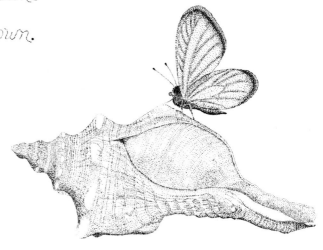

UNTITLED #7

As plants require the air and sun, our emotions require expression. If they are to thrive and be fulfilled, the language of the heart must be communicated. For, while love is often quiet, it is never silent.

Within your smile
I've found a world —
so rich in love,
so rare and fine —
that in its warmth
I choose to dwell
and share your life
and give you mine.

JASON

Jason is a special child. Medical science
has not found the way into his world, and
his mind seems to fly — — — like a butterfly
— — — in and out of the world we know.
Some day the key may be found, and we may
ease his quiet terrors and share the joys
that bring his frequent smiles.

UNTITLED #8

Suddenly, quietly, you realize that —
from this moment forth — you will no longer
pass through this world alone.
Like a new sun, this awareness rises within you,
freeing you from fear, opening your life.
This is the beginning of love
and the end of all that came before.

If, out of time,
I could lift one moment
and keep it shining,
always new;
of all the days
that I have lived,
I'd pick the moment
I first met you.

THE HARVEST OF A SOUL

The creation of a work of art is never accidental. It is the end result of an obsession to find that which is both true and beautiful within one's self or in the world we share. It is a conscious, slow and determined effort. It is the harvest of a soul.

UNTITLED #9

Love is elemental. Its nature is unselfish,
for it seeks only to nurture the life to which it is given.
With patience and tenderness it opens the way
for that life to grow, to unfurl and to dream.

Like the air,
  you sustain me.
Like the rain,
  you enrich me.
Like the sun,
  you warm me.
Like the night,
  you restore me.
You are the essence
  of my life.

THE CIRCLE OF THE SEASONS

Beyond the reach of calendars and clocks, the spirit of life glows within each of us — joining us, one to another, in an unbroken circle. In our origin and in our destiny we are one, and both the innocent and the wise embrace the whole.

OF GENTLE ACCORD

Friendship is a quiet joy. The words to express it
so often elude us, leaving us with only a silent smile.
Yet, on a sunny afternoon in Sausalito,
far from the one who filled my thoughts, I wrote this line,
and I knew that it would be understood.

No power on this earth
is so far beyond measure
nor so constant
and cherished
as the love of a friend.

THERE

This building was there. It is where I lived when I began to draw. Other people, too, thought of it as home. Some were born there; some died there. In March of 1979 I went back to photograph it for use in this drawing. Three weeks later I went back for more detailed photos. The building had been torn down. There isn't there anymore.

PARISIAN AUTUMN

Far away a calliope played, but its tune was broken in the cold,
wet wind. We sat beneath the barren sycamores. "Remember,"
you said, knowing I would. But did you know then
that, years away, I would remember it all — from May's
paper lanterns to November's pale light to the glint
of your plane as it etched the dark sky.

UNTITLED #10

Our spirits, too, are merged by love.
When we are separated physically by time and distance,
they remain entwined, joining the past we have shared
with the hope and promise of all that is yet to be.

Long after
our moments of closeness
have passed,
a part of you
remains with me
and warms the places
your hands have touched
and hastens my heart
for your return.

SPIRIT

This is an inward vision. Within each of us,
there is such a place. It is not an atmosphere
which reflects one's self-importance nor the span
of one's physical existence. It is the point at which
we recognize our union with that which is ever-
lasting, and it is a celebration of that love
and that wonder.

IN THE PRESENCE OF LOVE

*When love has entered our lives, there are
quiet signs that reveal its existence. These are not
self-conscious pronouncements. Rather, they are
subtle traces, revealing a new dimension of
warmth and joy both within us and without.*

LOCARNO, SWITZERLAND

*So many of the beauties of this earth
pass unnoticed. This shadow on the wall
of a building near the station caught my
gaze. I found with it a kind of spiritual
affinity, and, after returning to the
States, spent nearly fifty hours trying to
capture its haunting quality.*

TWO

The words on this work were the toast I gave
at the wedding of my brother, Tom, to his wife,
Cathy. Here, they are intended to celebrate
the love of two people for one another and the
wishes of those who are fortunate enough
to share in that pairing.

May every dawn
bring you joy.
May every sunset
bring you peace.
May all your days
be blessed
and brightened
by the love
you've come to share.

THE VOW

*In a time when nothing is more certain than change
the commitment of two people to one another
has become difficult and rare. Yet—by its scarcity—
the beauty and value of this exchange have only
been enhanced.*

... And we shall walk
    through all our days
        with love remembered and love renewed.